How Your BODY Works

Your
Senses

How Your
BODY
Works

Your
Senses

Anita Ganeri

Gareth Stevens Publishing
A WORLD ALMANAC EDUCATION GROUP COMPANY

ACKNOWLEDGMENTS

With thanks to: Lily Dang, Thomas Keen, Billy Hart, Nicola Mooi, Charlie Summerford, Kelsey Sharman, Sophie Raven, Gurlaine Kaur-Sidhu, Kyle Bradley-Murfet, Elmaz Ekram, Diandra Beckles. Models from Truly Scrumptious Ltd.

Please visit our web site at: www.garethstevens.com
For a free color catalog describing Gareth Stevens Publishing's
list of high-quality books and multimedia programs, call
1-800-542-2595 (USA) or 1-800-387-3178 (Canada).
Gareth Stevens Publishing's fax: (414) 332-3567.

Library of Congress Cataloging-in-Publication Data

Ganeri, Anita, 1961-
    Your senses / by Anita Ganeri.
        p. cm. — (How your body works)
    Summary: Discusses the five senses and how they work.
    Includes bibliographical references and index.
    ISBN 0-8368-3636-7 (lib. bdg.)
    1. Senses and sensation—Juvenile literature.   [1. Senses and sensation.]   I. Title.   II. Series.
    QP434.G36   2003
    612.8—dc21   2002036532

This North American edition first published in 2003 by
Gareth Stevens Publishing
A World Almanac Education Group Company
330 West Olive Street, Suite 100
Milwaukee, WI 53212 USA

Original edition © 2003 by Evans Brothers Limited. First published in 2003 by Evans Brothers Limited, 2A Portman Mansions, Chiltern Street, London W1U 6NR, United Kingdom. This U.S. edition published under license from Evans Brothers Limited. This U.S. edition © 2003 by Gareth Stevens, Inc. Additional end matter © 2003 by Gareth Stevens, Inc.

Designer: Mark Holt
Artwork: Julian Baker
Photography: Steve Shott
Consultant: Dr. M. Turner

Gareth Stevens Editor: Carol Ryback
Gareth Stevens Designer: Katherine A. Goedheer

Photo credits:
Science Photo Library: Omikron, page 12; Quest, page 16; Omikron, page 20; Quest, page 23; Chris Bjornberg, page 24. Bruce Coleman Collection: page 14, page 16.

Printed in the United States of America

1 2 3 4 5 6 7 8 9 07 06 05 04 03

Contents

Making Sense

How do you know what is going on around you? Your five **senses** tell you. Your senses send messages from your eyes, ears, nose, mouth, and skin to your brain to tell you about the world around you.

Your senses of smell and taste work together. If you have a stuffy nose, even yummy ice cream can taste like boring cardboard!

Your five senses are seeing, hearing, smelling, tasting, and touching.

You feel things with your skin. It tells you what is rough or smooth, hot or cold, or painful.

You smell things with your nose. You can sniff the air to smell your supper cooking in the kitchen.

You hear things with your two ears. Ears pick up all kinds of sounds.

You taste things with your tongue. It has tiny bumps that hold special taste buds.

You see things with your eyes. You see in black and white and in color.

Messages from Outside

Each of your senses is linked to your brain. Your brain is the most important part of your body. Your brain makes sense of what is going on around you. As you read this book, **nerves** in your eyes send messages about the words and pictures to your brain. Your brain then sorts the messages and tells you what you are seeing. Your amazing brain also tells your fingers to turn the page after you have finished reading.

Your hard, bony skull protects your amazing brain. Gently knock on your head to feel your hard, bony skull.

You have about 100 million nerves running through your body. Some nerves carry messages from your five senses to your brain. Other nerves carry messages the other way, from your brain to your body. Nerves can also send messages to one another. This nerve network helps you understand what is happening outside your body. Your nerves and brain form your **nervous system**.

Amazing!
Every minute, millions and millions of nerve messages whiz around your body.

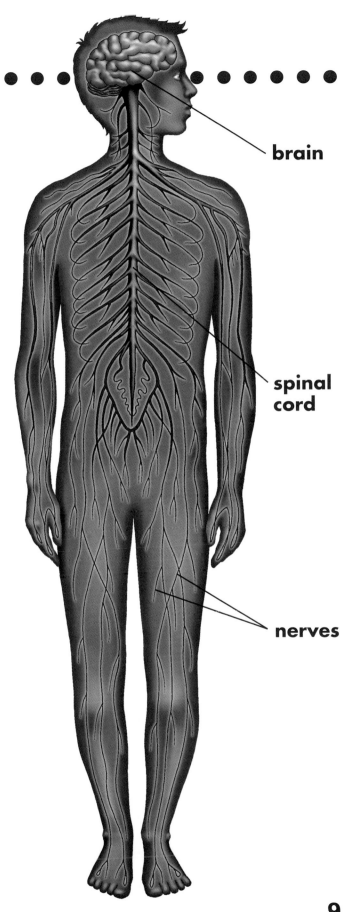

brain

spinal cord

nerves

Eye Spy

Look at your eyes in a mirror. See the two tiny, black dots in the middle of them? These are your **pupils**. Pupils are really holes that let light into your eyes. Your eyes need light to see. That's why you cannot see things very well in the dark.

Carrots contain a substance called **vitamin** A that helps the cells in your eyes pick up light.

Light bounces off objects and sends a picture message, or image, into your eyes. Special nerves in your eyes send the image to your brain. The image that your nerves send to your brain is upside down. Your amazing brain flips the image right-side-up and tells you what you are seeing. Each part of your eye has a different but important job to do.

Amazing!

Your eyelashes help keep irritating dust and dirt out of your eyes.

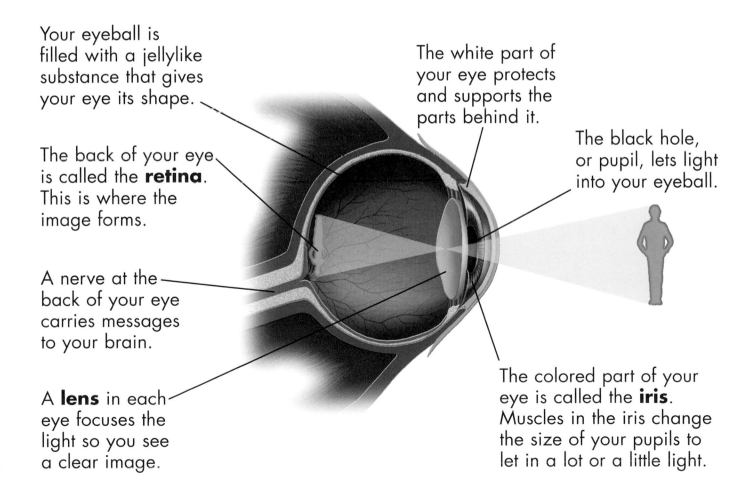

Your eyeball is filled with a jellylike substance that gives your eye its shape.

The back of your eye is called the **retina**. This is where the image forms.

A nerve at the back of your eye carries messages to your brain.

A **lens** in each eye focuses the light so you see a clear image.

The white part of your eye protects and supports the parts behind it.

The black hole, or pupil, lets light into your eyeball.

The colored part of your eye is called the **iris**. Muscles in the iris change the size of your pupils to let in a lot or a little light.

More about Eyes

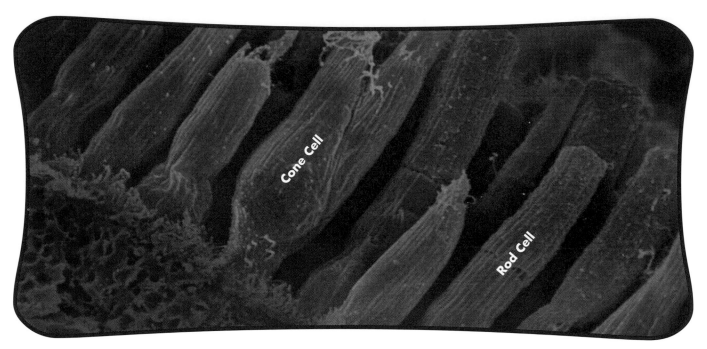

Rod cells and cone cells in your retina are shaped like rods and cones.

Tiny nerve cells in the back of your eyes pick up the light that shines into them. These nerve cells are called **rods** and **cones**. Rods help you see in black and white and in dim light. Cones help you see colors. Cones work best in bright light. That is why colors seem to fade or change to gray at night.

Some people are **color-blind**. The cone cells in their eyes do not work right. People who are color-blind cannot tell the difference between certain colors.

Amazing!
Your iris can be blue, brown, hazel, gray, green, or even red. You get your eye color from your parents. What color are your eyes?

Do you wear glasses to help you see clearly? Some people need glasses to help them see close up or far away. Without glasses, the images they see look fuzzy. Glasses are extra lenses. They help the lenses inside your eyes focus the light that comes into them.

Two eyes give you a better view of the world than just one eye. Try it yourself: shut one eye, then the other.

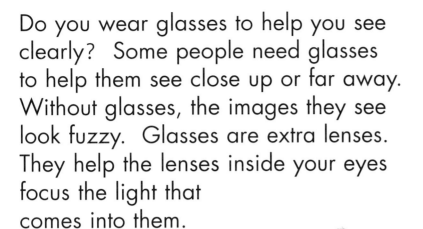

Ear, Ear

Your outer ears work somewhat like funnels. Their funnel shape is very useful for catching all the different sounds from the air. As sound enters your funnel-shaped ears, it quickly travels to the ear parts deep inside your head.

Some animals, such as rabbits, move their ears to help catch sounds. Can you wiggle your ears, too?

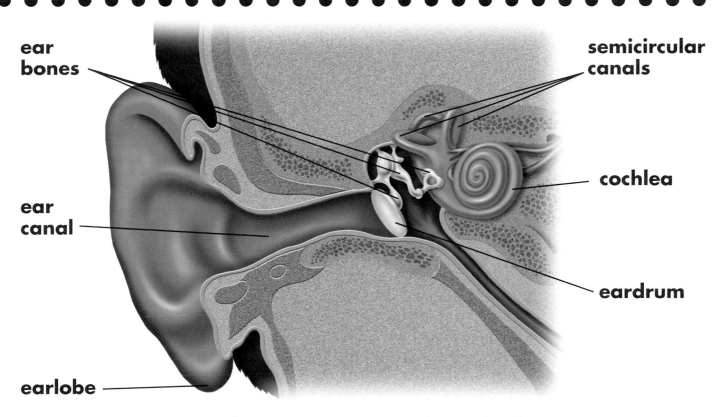

ear bones

semicircular canals

ear canal

cochlea

earlobe

eardrum

You have many ear parts inside your head.

Sound travels down your ear canal until it hits a thin, tight skin called your **eardrum**. Sound makes your eardrum move back and forth, or **vibrate**. As your eardrum vibrates, it jiggles three very tiny ear bones. The vibrating bones send sound to an ear part called your **cochlea**. Inside your cochlea, sound shakes some **hairy nerves** that send messages to your brain. Your brain tells you what you hear.

Amazing!

The tiny bones inside your ears are the smallest bones in your body. They are about the same size as grains of rice.

More about Ears

Why do you think you have two ears? You have two ears so you can tell which direction sound is coming from. Sound will enter one of your ears just before it enters the other. The sound that gets to your brain first seems louder — and closer — to you.

Your amazing ears can hear sounds as quiet as a person whispering or as loud as an airplane. Your ears can also hear high sounds and low sounds. High sounds make the air vibrate very fast. Low sounds make the air vibrate more slowly.

Amazing!

Some animals, such as bats and dogs, have amazing hearing. They hear high sounds that people never even notice at all.

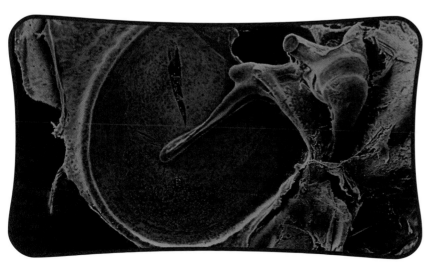
Your eardrum vibrates when sound hits it.

Your ears also help you balance. Deep in each ear are three tiny tubes called **semicircular canals**. Each canal points in a different direction — forward, backward, or sideways. As you move, liquid inside the canals tickles some special nerve cells that have tiny hairs. These hairy nerves send messages to your brain to keep your body steady and in balance.

As ballet dancers spin around, they turn their heads to keep their eyes on the same spot. This stops them from feeling dizzy.

What's That Smell?

Some things smell nice, such as a bunch of flowers or a freshly baked cake. Other things smell terrible, like stinky socks or milk that has spoiled. Smells float in the air, but they are too small to see. Your nose senses these smells and sends messages about them to your brain.

Pinching your nostrils helps keep you from smelling bad smells.

18

When you breathe in, smells in the air go up your nose. Special hairy nerves inside your nose soak up the smells and send messages about them to your brain. Your amazing brain tells you what you are smelling.

Sniffing makes a smell seem stronger. Usually, when you breathe, you only take in a little air. But when you sniff hard, you take in more air, and the smells go straight to your nose nerves.

Amazing!

You can smell more than three thousand different smells, but a dog can smell about three billion!

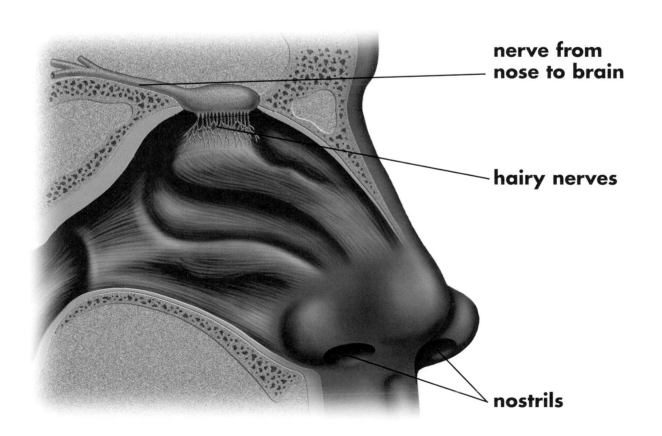

nerve from
nose to brain

hairy nerves

nostrils

Tastes Good

● ●

You taste sweet, salty, sour, and bitter foods with your tongue. It is covered with tiny bumps that contain special cells called **taste buds**. Your taste buds send messages along nerves to your brain to tell you what you are eating. Your tongue also tells you if your food is too hot, too cold, or just right.

Look in a mirror and stick out your tongue. The tiny bumps on the surface of your tongue hold your taste buds.

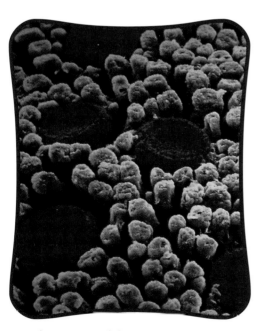

Flat, round bumps on your tongue hold your taste buds. A special **microscope** took this picture.

Your tongue is a muscle that twists and turns many different ways so you can taste, talk, and sing. It also helps you eat by moving your food around your mouth so your teeth can chew it. Then, your tongue pushes the food toward the back of your mouth so you can swallow it.

Amazing!

You have more than 10,000 taste buds on your tongue. Each of your taste buds lives about one week.

Touchy, Feely

You touch and feel things with your skin. As your skin touches objects around you, it tells you if they are hot, cold, soft, hard, rough, or smooth. Your skin also feels pain.

Your skin covers your whole body. It fits your body perfectly and bends and stretches when you move. Skin holds your insides in. Millions of tiny nerves are packed under your skin. The nerves send messages to your brain to tell you what you are touching or feeling.

The skin on your fingertips is very **sensitive**. That is why petting a cat feels soft and warm.

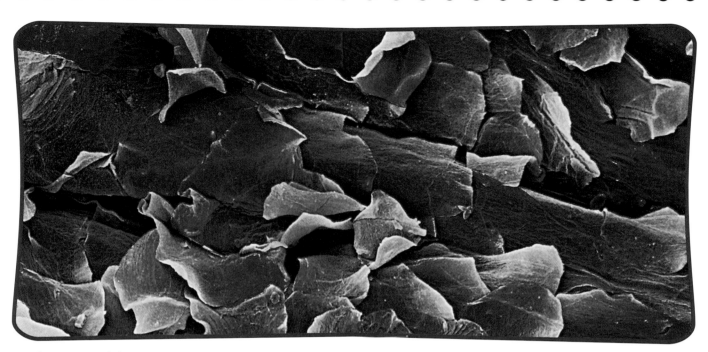

If you could see the surface of your skin very close up, it would look like corn flakes.

Amazing!

Pricking your finger causes pain, but pain is useful. Pain warns you that something is wrong, so you can keep from getting hurt even more.

Every second, nerves in your skin send thousands of messages to your brain. But your skin is not equally sensitive all over your body. Areas of your skin with lots of nerves packed close to each other are more sensitive to touch. Your eyelids, lips, and fingertips are very sensitive skin areas with lots of nerves. Areas of your skin with fewer nerves spread farther apart are not as sensitive. Skin on the palms of your hands, your back, or your legs is less sensitive to touch.

More about Skin

In addition to feeling and touching, your skin has many other important jobs. Your skin protects your body from harm. It helps keep you warm on cold days and cool on hot days. It mends itself when you get cut or scratched. Your skin is also covered with a very thin coat of oil. This oil coating makes your skin smooth and waterproof. That is why you don't get soggy when you go swimming!

Use a magnifying glass to look at your fingertips. Can you see your **fingerprints**?

No one else has the same fingerprints as you.

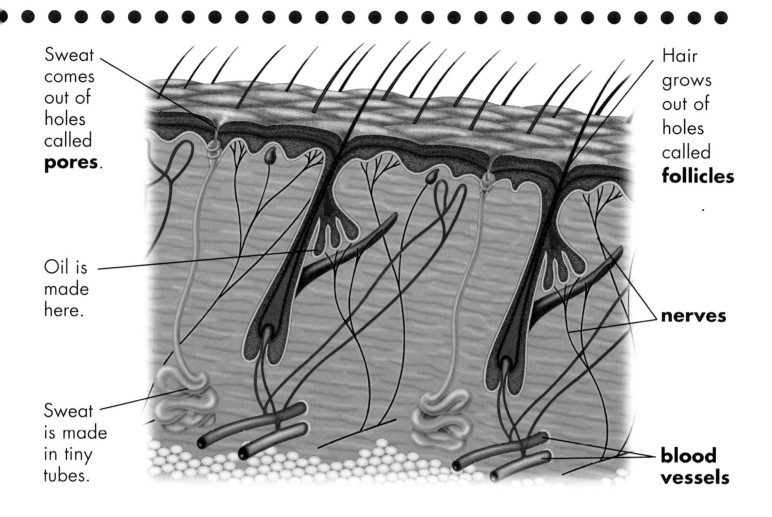

Sweat comes out of holes called **pores**.

Oil is made here.

Sweat is made in tiny tubes.

Hair grows out of holes called **follicles**

nerves

blood vessels

Lots of things happen inside your amazing skin. Hair grows from tiny holes in your skin. Other holes make salty sweat. Tiny tubes, called **blood vessels**, bring blood to your skin. Blood brings your skin oxygen from the air you breathe and **nutrients** from the food you eat.

Amazing!

The thickest skin on your body grows on the soles of your feet. The thinnest skin grows on your delicate eyelids.

Activity

Your ear has many different parts. How many parts can you name? Photocopy page 27. Match the numbers below to the ear parts listed on page 27.

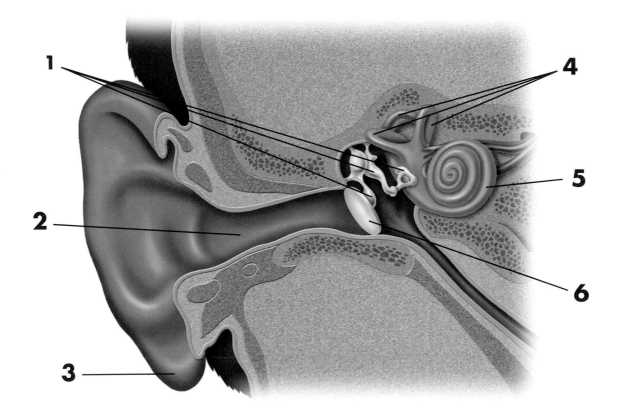

____ **earlobe**

____ **eardrum**

____ **ear canal**

____ **ear bones**

____ **cochlea**

____ **semicircular canals**

Glossary

blood vessels: soft, flexible "tubes" that carry blood to every area of your body.

cochlea: a snail-shaped inner ear structure that contains hairy nerves that send sounds to your brain.

color-blind: lacking the type of cone cells that help you see certain colors.

cones: special nerve cells in the retina of your eye that help you see colors.

eardrum: a very thin, tight skin that stretches across the end of your ear canal.

fingerprints: tiny ridges that form a special pattern of lines, circles, or loops on the inside tips of your fingers. You also have toeprints.

follicles: tiny holes in your skin that hair grows out of.

hairy nerves: a special type of sensory nerves found in your ears and nose that use tiny hairs to help feel things.

iris: the colored part of your eye that automatically changes size to control the amount of light entering your eyeball.

lens: the clear disk inside your eye that focuses light so you can see clearly.

microscope: an instrument used to look at objects that are too tiny to see using just your eyes alone.

nerves: special cells that carry messages between your body and your brain. They look like very tiny wires or threads.

nervous system: the network formed by your brain and all the nerves in your body.

nutrients: tiny pieces of food that are carried around your body by your blood.

pores: very tiny holes in your skin that produce sweat to help cool you or oil to help your skin stay soft.

pupils: the black dots in the middle of your eyes that let light into your eyeballs.

retina: the inside lining of your eyeball that contains special nerve cells such as rods and cones.

rods: special nerve cells in the retina of your eye that help you see in black and white and in dim light.

semicircular canals: the tiny tubes inside your head that help you keep your balance.

senses: the five different ways your body tells you about the world around you. Your five senses are seeing, hearing, smelling, tasting, and touching.

sensitive: able to use any, some, or all of your five senses to discover what is happening around you.

taste buds: special nerve cells on your tongue that help you taste different flavors.

vibrate: to move quickly back and forth or side to side.

vitamin: an important element in your food that helps your body stay healthy and strong.

More Books to Read

How Do I Know It's Yucky?
And Other Questions about
the Senses. Body Wise (series).
Sharon Cromwell (Heinemann)

My Eyes Are for Seeing. My
Five Senses (series). Jane Belk
Moncure (Child's World)

My Five Senses. Let's-Read-and-
Find-Out Science (series). Aliki
(HarperTrophy)

The Science of the Senses.
Living Science (series).
Patricia Miller-Schroeder
(Gareth Stevens)

Sense-Abilities: Fun Ways
to Explore the Senses.
Michelle O'Brien-Palmer
(Chicago Review Press)

Smelling and Tasting. What
About (series). Lesley Sims
(Raintree/Steck-Vaughn)

Videos

Bear in Big Blue House: Sense
Sational. (Columbia Tristar)

Zoboomafoo: Sense-Sational
Animal Friends. (PBS)

Web Sites

BrainPOP: Vision.
www.brainpop.com/health/
senses/vision/

The Magic School Bus Gets an
Earful. place.scholastic.com/
magicschoolbus/games/sound/

Index